I Know Your Cry: an Adoption Story

by

Larry A. Yff

CHAPTERS

INTRODUCTION

Should I have an abortion or give my baby up for adoption? If I kill my baby, will I be able to live with that? If I give my baby up to be raised by someone else and he resents me when he is older, will I be able to live with that?

That dilemma, and its' answers, have been around since the beginning of human civilization. The world as we know it has been shaped and affected by abortions and adoptions.

My story, thank God, has been shaped by adoption...

CHAPTER ONE

<u>Give it up</u>

"...I heard you crying down the hall. I knew it was you. You were crying because you had just been circumcised. I had heard that other mothers can tell when it's their child who is crying, but I did not believe it until...until the nurses brought you to me. They weren't supposed to bring you to me because I had already signed you up for adoption, but they made a mistake, brought you to me and laid you on my chest...you immediately stopped crying and went to sleep. My heart melted. Once they realized their mistake, they came and took you from me. They practically ripped you from my arms and you began to cry. Then I cried. We both were crying. I changed my mind. You didn't have a choice. I didn't want to give you up anymore and you didn't want me to let you go anymore. I had felt your heartbeat against mine and I wanted that feeling to last forever…"

Those were the words from a letter my biological mom sent me. She was 17 years old at the time. She had already had a daughter and had given her up for adoption and now she caught herself in the same cycle, forced to make the same decision with the same man, the young father of her 2 children.

She sent me that letter during some communication we recently had. I was curious to know a little more about her and she told me writing was in my blood because she had started to write what was possibly going to be a book. The excerpt you read was from her writing not-yet-turned-book titled "It wasn't you".

At 1st glance, you may think she was irresponsible and an unfit mother. If you thought that, you would be partially correct, in my eyes. In my eyes, yes, she was an unfit mother at that time…but why? We all have our reasons and rationales for what we do. We seldom, if ever, do something just because we felt like doing it.

Her letter gave me insight into her decision. She was young and in love, or at least "in like" with my biological dad. Young people have sex. They have sex with "people they aren't supposed to" sometimes. Sometimes they have sex when they're not supposed to and other times, they have sex when they have no ideal what they're really getting into.

Does that make my biological mom, wait a minute…I'm not going to keep typing "biological mom" and "biological dad." Her name is Zohra and his name is Kelvin. There. That will make it much easier for me to write and for you to keep up. Now, let's get back to irresponsible Zohra…

Guilty. Guilty as charged. Any family court would find her to be 100% guilty and irresponsible on all charges. Does that mean she didn't love me? Does that mean we as a society should judge her and not help her; especially since she made the same "mistake" twice in 2 years?

I would encourage all parents who gave their child or children up for adoption or have lost kids due to situations in your life to write one. Write a "It wasn't you" letter. It helps. It bonds. It clarifies a whole lot of shit. Does this mean the court's ruling and society's judgement about you will be overridden? No, but it will help you get a better sentence from them if they knew more about you and viewed you as a human and not a number or a court case.

I have to admit, I didn't think too highly of Zohra when I was growing up, but to be fair, I didn't really think about her at all growing up. I was in a stable home that had mom and dad present every day. Dad took care of the bills and always had a job; while mom had breakfast ready at 7am every morning, dinner at 5pm sharp and got all the kids in bed promptly by 8pm (I think we could stay up until 9pm on the weekends) every day.

I had a mom so Zohra didn't matter to me. She was simply my egg donor, much like some women get mad and reduce the father of their kids to just being "that sperm donor."

In my eyes, a mom was a female who took care of the kids and was married to her husband. She was the nurturer and he was the provider. She took care of the house and he made sure she had a house to take care of.

Zohra became a factor when I began to make black friends. I would watch them get into actual fights when somebody would joke to much about someone else's mom. I never understood that and they never understood why I didn't understand them.

"Why can't you talk about somebody's mom?" I would ask. Their reply was typically something like, "Why do you call her mom? Don't no black kids call their mamas 'mom'. And you're basically white anyways, so a mama is different to you. Just leave it alone. You wouldn't understand."

Those are the conversations and things I was having and learning about when I was growing up. Being adopted by white parents gave me an *interesting* view on what a parent was. I was learning that a white mom was different than a black mama. What was my black mom like?

This was the stage in my life where my curiosity in my black mom was sparked. I wanted to have that bond my black friends had with their moms to the point where I would be willing to fight to the death to protect my mom or even to protect anyone from telling "yo mama jokes" about her, but I wasn't there yet. I wasn't in that space and didn't know how to get there.

I remember feeling lonely but not lonely enough to dig too deep into this black mom stuff. I had a mom. I knew my mom loved me and I loved her. I knew my mom was white and that I was black and based on that fact, I also assumed she did not birth me and that was good enough for me.

In my early years up until I was around 19, I was content to just leave it alone and enjoy my white mom. Who needs a black mom anyways? They sound violent!

I was hearing stories of my black friends who got beatings from their moms with extension cords and small tree branches! If that's what having a black mom was all about...I'll *definitely* stick with my white mom! White moms gave their kids spankings.

For those of you unfamiliar with what a spanking is, a spanking is when you have to bend over and get spanked on your ass with a hand or a ruler...never a belt or an extension cord.

Getting a spanking is still a disciplinary act, but it's an act that is based on a mutual and implied understanding. That understanding is the spanking was mandatory for making a mistake and it will occur again whenever you make that same mistake until you learn your lesson.

Both parties, the spanker and the spankee, both know there is no ill intention in a spanking. It's just business and once business is taken care of, it's back to being a cohesive family unit. Not so much with reprimands by black mamas...

From what I heard, there is a whole lot of name-calling, screaming, crying, paranoia and fear surrounding "spankings" from a black mom! A black mom "didn't play that shit!" When she said it was time for bed, you had to go to bed. No negotiations. No discussions. No talking back. Your only option is to go to bed.

In the cases where it was time for a spanking with my white mom, it was an orderly affair. She would let you know, just in case you weren't aware or had forgotten, that it was time for your spanking. At that time, in my family, that meant taking that dreaded walk.

When it was spanking time, you had to walk upstairs and wait. And wait. And wait. At some point, you would hear the footsteps of my white mom approach the bottom stair, land on the 1st stair, step on the landing and continue up those stairs until she was in sight. At that point your heart would race, just a little, until she arrived at the top of the second set of stairs where you sat, patiently waiting, and escorted you into her room.

At that point, the room went from the "honeymoon suite" to the disciplinary wing of a prison. You would take your place at the foot of the bed while you watched her grab her trusty yardstick out of the closet, your heart rate would increase a little more and the reality of what was coming next would sit in.

White mom would then turn towards you. That was your cue. That was the mutually agreed upon signal to loosen your belt, let your pants fall to the floor and bend over the bed.

Smack! Smack! Smack! "Have you learned your lesson yet?", my white mom would ask. Through my tears I would say, "Yes" only to still get one or two more Smacks!

Spankings had a clear beginning and an ending with my white mom…not so much with black moms. I've heard the instant a black son, for instance, knows he has crossed some imaginary, but very real line, an instant panic and fear sets in. This process wasn't a gradual thing that crescendoed into the expected level of dread, because there *was no level* of expected dread. The level of anticipation and panic typically rose straight to the High Alert level, bypassing all the levels one might expect while waiting for a white mom spanking.

From what I gathered, this was because each "black mama spanking" was unique and instilled its' own, mixed level of fear, love and understanding each time. One time you may be in public so the in-store "spanking" is like a test run, with the real deal happening sometime between exiting the store and getting home.

The real spanking might involve, like I mentioned earlier, a belt or anything that was shaped like a belt; while other times, it just might mean you got cussed out. Then there were the times where you would get the belt and a cussing out.

I've heard stories of black moms actually chasing their intended target down the street, catching up to him or her and using her hand to spank and/or smack and/or choke her child into compliance at which time the child would respectfully take his or her punishment, while screaming "I'm sorry mama!" and then walk back home alongside black mom.

The endings of black mom spankings weren't clearly defined either from what I could tell. Even after enduring all that pain and punishment in an event like the one where black mom had to chase you, my black friends would still tell me how, usually just before you both entered the house, black mom would deliver a crisp Smack! to the back of the head with a clear warning that, among other things, she "better not never in her life ever have to chase your ass down the street like that again or next time it will be worse". Worse!?!?

Here's the bottom line of all that: I had a mom. I was content. My white mom and me had a stable, loving mom-son relationship and I was content. And anyways, my biological mom gave me up. She gave me up so it doesn't matter. Nothing about her and I matter because she decided to "give *it* up for adoption."

CHAPTER TWO

<u>My Black Baby Mamas</u>

I had my 1st child when I was 19 years old. His mom is black. I used to seriously joke and say she was mixed: half black and half crazy, but it was true and something about that crazy held my attention…

I was fresh out of graduating from the local, all-white Christian high-school when he was born. My interactions with black people were extremely limited and had not included sexual interactions with black females except for with his mom at this point. Wait! I lied…

The summer I met his mom, my parents left me Home Alone for about a month while they went to California. I used that opportunity to do like the little boy in the movie Home Alone did, but not to get into mischief…I used that time to get *into* black females.

You know what? Before I even got to that part of the story, we still have to backtrack about 2 years. During my 2nd year of high school, I got anxious. I had seen black girls up-close at basketball and football games when my high school would play black high schools. I needed to get a closer look…

There was a black high school about 2 blocks from mine and I would sneak over there at lunch times or after school and freely wander around and observe "black people in their natural environment." I liked it. To be more specific, *I liked the black girls*!

I could move freely at that high school after school, but it was *during* school hours that was the problem. They had security guards and these guards could pretty much spot me as an outsider. I was the one with the slightly *goofy* walk, the wide-eyed look like I was walking through a museum or zoo and I had my blue jeans rolled up at the bottom white-boy style.

Upon seeing me, they would ask me for a school identification card that they knew I couldn't produce and kick me off the premises. I wasn't worried about them too much and continued my "black tours" until they threatened to contact my school or the local authorities and book me for trespassing and *that's almost* where we pick up the story about my 1st child's mom.

I said almost because during the month my parents left me Home Alone, I had sex with a "couple" of black girls. Details about who they were I will leave out because it could make them easily identifiable BUT I will say this: most of them knew each other.

One of them said she was curious about me because I was black but I wasn't really black. Her sister would come across my plate next. Another black girl who knew the 1st one would come by for her "experiment" with her 1st "white-black-boy" and then the final episode was stopped during the showing. I don't remember

why. Fine. I lied again. I *do* remember why: it wasn't what she

expected.

Wasn't what she expected? I didn't know we were getting

into any of this with any kind of expectation. I thought it was what

it was until it wasn't. Apparently, and yes, I am man enough to

admit it, she said I didn't "sex her like a black man is supposed to",

so, like I mentioned, she cut the episode short. *Now* we can circle

back and get into the part of the story about my oldest child's

mama...

She was everything I had heard about, saw on television and

read about in books: a black mama! I think what I liked about it

was the fact that I was able to get my 1st black mama experiences

in 2nd hand. By 2nd hand I mean, it wasn't *my* black mama

interacting with me. I was able to kind of sit on the sidelines and

watch it all unfold from a safe distance.

To be honest, I was jealous. I was jealous of the experiences my son was having with his black mom. He was probably jealous of my sideline position and on many occasions, he probably wished we could switch places.

He interacted differently with his black mom than I did with my white mom. The differences weren't something the untrained eye could easily pick up. You would have had to either been black and adopted at birth into a white family or been the white parents who adopted a black child at birth in order to pick up on the subtleties.

Let me slow down and clarify some things before we go on. I love my white mom and I am in no way saying she didn't know how to discipline me or show me love. She had her style just like all mothers have their own styles. I am simply stating, appreciating and showing the difference in the mom-son relationships I experienced and saw and that are in society.

Tameka. That is the name of my oldest child's mama. Actually, it's not Tameka, but I don't want to put all of her business and name out there. If you know her, you know her...if you don't, you don't. And if you don't know her, just be content to call her 'Tameka' or 'Meka' for short, okay? Cool...

So, Tameka disciplined her child in what I would describe as a powerful, loving, dominating, reassuring way. She got it honestly because she got it from her mama. Tameka and I lived with her mom for a while and that was my 1st first-hand interaction with a black mom.

Apparently, when Tameka's mom was younger, she was known for taking no shit. If you had something to say to her, be direct. Don't beat around the bush because if you did, she would beat that ass. Give her respect and she will give you respect. If you disrespect her or her kids, then she will disrespect you. Her parenting style and attitude towards me reflected this view and Meka parented with the same mentality.

When our son needed discipline, he knew it, I knew it and she knew it. We were all on the same page in that sense, but he was the only one who physically felt it. It was weird watching him get disciplined and being jealous of him.

Her black mom disciplinary style gave him a level of love, fear and respect that was different than what I had experienced with my mom. Once again, it's a hard thing to explain, but I'll try...

During slavery, yes, everything in America tends to circle back to slavery, black parents had to teach their kids at an extremely young age about white people. They had to teach their kids that the law of the land in both notion and actual, governmental legislation said all white people were superior to black people in every way.

The young black kids were taught at an early age that they should never, under any circumstance, talk back or question any white person, especially a white male. To do so would mean he had the legal right to physically beat you or kill you without punishment from the American court system.

With this in mind, black parents preferred to beat this vital lesson into their kids in a loving, but intentional, way. The common thought was it would be better for them, the parent, to aggressively teach their children the prejudicial realities of the day so that their children take their racial lessons seriously. Not taking those lessons seriously would result in death or imprisonment 99% of the time. Last point tying black parenting style to slavery...

The black woman was in charge of the house. She systematically became the cornerstone of the family. She was the stable one. She was the disciplinarian. She was what we call the "strong, black woman". She wasn't this way by choice.

While she was being preserved for breeding and maintaining stability in the black family, the white slave master and white society in general during that era in America, were busy with the business of enslaving, imprisoning and killing black males. They

weren't afforded the luxuries of a stable life for generations.

It was the role of the black male to work the fields as a slave

from sun-up until sun-down. It was the role of the black man to be

submissive to white people.   It was the goal of white people,

particularly the white males, to apply their government, man-made

right of superiority and deliver that message home to the black

males in any way possible. Murder, hangings, lynching's and other

gruesome tactics were standard and par for the course in instilling

this frame of mind.

And that's where we have the birth of the "strong, black,

disciplinary, no-nonsense black mama." The responsibility to teach

young, black children was laid upon her shoulders. She became the

1st line of defense against unnecessary attacks and harm, physical

and mental, from white people for her children. If she did not instill

the importance of understanding how to navigate a racially divided

system in America, not only would her children be killed...the entire next generations would not exist. They would all be killed off or forced to live a life of slavery.

That is where we are at when we get back into my understanding of black mom. She had to be hard. She had to lovingly beat her kids into submission and for doing so, she got the love and respect for saving their lives and the future of black Americans.

"Don't ever talk about my mama! After all she went through and handled her business...don't disrespect her! I will kill you for that!" I was beginning to understand it now.

My son was learning 1st hand, without all of the background, historical information I was privy to. That information wouldn't have done him any good anyways. Whether he knew his history or not, when it was time for Tameka to discipline him, he was gonna get it regardless.

I was still jealous. Why? Did I want Tameka to beat my ass? No! Absolutely not! Did she ever get mad enough to try? Yes! Absolutely yes! Did I mind? No. I didn't mind. I sensed there was something below the surface in all black moms that I could never relate to. I just knew that whatever it was, it provided the energy for their disciplinary engines as well as their entire outlook on life.

In a weird way, I appreciated her style of showing me love or at least emotion. It had a soothing effect somehow. It was something I never had...but I still missed it. How is that possible? How is it possible to miss something you never had?

I was intrigued. Did my son realize the level of love he was getting every time he would get in trouble? I was sure that he didn't understand it because I was sure his black mom didn't understand it. It was just a "thing" black moms did. It was just a "thing" all black women had in common.

Some understood it; while others simply imitated their mothers. Either way, this "thing" worked back in the day and continues to work today in the majority of black homes, in my view.

As I would move on with life, I would amass a whopping 6 "baby mamas", resulting in 6 kids. Did I feel guilty? Did I intentionally go it because of some sort of crazy addiction to Black Mom Love?

To be honest with you, the guilt of not being there for my older kids and their mothers while they were growing up didn't hit me until I had to face my addictions and that is an entirely different story for an entirely different book. To be specific, that book is called "White, Confused, Black and Christian – the Autobiography of Larry A. Yff" (base or explicit version).

I won't go down that path with you here, but I do need you to know that all of my interactions with my "black, baby mamas" and their mamas starting with Tameka, begin to tug at me a little more with each relationship. The tug I was feeling was an internal

longing to find my black mom and experience that all important

aspect of what I thought being black as all about: experiencing

Black Mom Love.

CHAPTER THREE

<u>Meeting my Black Mom</u>

I was adopted at birth into a white family. I was beginning to understand the different family structures in America that white families had versus black families. There were definite differences...not excuses or claims for racial superiority. Just differences.

Along with these differences in family structure came differences in parenting styles. The mom's position in black and white families were different but equal. I'm telling you this based on what I have heard, not from what I actually knew, until...until I met my black mom...

I had the wonderful opportunity to meet my biological mom and sisters. How that came about was crazy! And yes, I'm about to tell you...

I wrote a letter to the adoption agency in New Jersey where I was born, inquiring about where my birth mom was at as well as a sister I had. This took place when I was around 21 years old. That exact day, they received the one and only phone call my older, biological sister made to that same agency. We were connected to each other.

Her name is Carol. She was given up for adoption at birth prior to me being born. Her adoption story is completely different than mine. In fact, her adoption story shaped her view of my mother in a completely different light than I did. We might get into that a little later on in the story. For now, let's focus on our initial meeting…

I get Carol's phone number and call her. We chat for a while and I asked a couple of questions about our mom. She said, "Hold on for a second." Next thing I know, I hear a female voice on the other line saying, "Hello? Hello?" It was Zohra. It was my 1st time hearing the voice of the woman who was responsible for both my birth and my confused life as a black man.

I was silent. What was I supposed to say? What was she supposed to say? Who was supposed to talk 1st? Carol interrupted the silence by telling me to say "hello" to *my* mom. And by "my" she was referring to me. I say "Hello."

Carol had to referee the 1st couple of minutes and explain to an unexpecting Zohra, that the son she had given up for adoption 21 years ago was on the phone and he was saying "hello" to her. After another awkward silence, Carol broke it again and told us to exchange numbers and call each other later. We did what she told us to do.

After Carol and I talked some more, I would have my 1st real conversation with my black mom. This is what I wanted right? I was telling myself that this could be the answer to a lot of my addictions and life issues. Talking to her would be the secret sauce that would help me appreciate my children's mom in a new and enlightening way. A way that I never knew existed until now! My life was about to dramatically change for the better and I was excited!

If I could make the sound of the air coming out of a balloon right here, I would. That sound would represent the sunny thoughts I had about meeting my black mom. It would represent the fact that meeting her was not the life-changing event I thought it would be. I would even describe it as being a non-life-changing, non-life-improving, non-essential life event at the time.

We would talk several times on the phone and get acquainted as much as 2 strangers could who were put in a phone booth together. What happened? I was finally in contact with my black mom and I didn't feel any blacker? I didn't feel any new revelations in my life that would make me treat my children and their mom's any differently.

Eventually, she would take a trip to Michigan and we would all meet up in person. By "we" I mean, her, my adoptive parents and my big sister I grew up with who was also adopted at birth into the same family.

I was happy meeting her in the flesh. Even though it was much better than just talking to her on the phone, it still didn't feel like she was my mom. I had a mom. I had a white mom. I was content, remember?

The introduction of Zohra into my life caused as much confusion as it did calm. What do I call her? Do I tell people she is my "black mom"? Do I now call my adopted mom my "white mom"? Now that I know her, am I supposed to cling to her and protect her like black sons do with their mamas? Do I call her Zohra or mama or mom?

As you can tell, meeting her raised a ton of questions for me. I pressed in as best as I could and called her mom. I called her mom and she called me "Adam". More confusion.

Apparently, she had named me at birth and thought the name she gave me, Adam Troy Khan, was officially and legally on my birth certificate. Now *she* was confused!

We would continue to talk off and on for years with a casual bond that grew into a polite, semi-formal bond. It was a place we were both comfortable operating in until...until I got the "It wasn't you" letter. That was the game-changer!

This letter not only told me that my being adopted wasn't my fault, it had nothing to do with me and everything to do with her. This was a reassuring letter that didn't change my view on her in the way you would think.

It didn't make me not think it was my fault anymore, because I never thought it was my fault. I never thought it was her fault. I never thought it was anybody's fault. I never thought about it past the point of "I have a black mom somewhere and she put me up for adoption." Adoption to me was simply a process that took me from one situation to another. It was a process that gave me a mom and dad because my mom and dad, for whatever reason or reasons, "enrolled" me for adoption.

In this letter, I, for the 1st time in my life, viewed Zohra as both a human and a mom. Until that letter, she was a mom by default. She was a mom because she had children. That letter made her a mom because she had me "in her tummy" for 9 months and made the decision to give me up for adoption because she wasn't ready to handle the responsibilities of motherhood.

I learned that she was young and irresponsible like a lot of young kids. I could relate to her. I was irresponsible and had kids at stages in my life where I was not mentally, spiritually or financially able to be a constant figure in their lives. I never viewed myself as being worthless...just irresponsible.

Zohra wasn't worthless either…just irresponsible. She was irresponsible twice. She had my older sister Carol and gave her up for adoption, turned around and got in the same situation and less than a year later, gave her next child, me, up for adoption.

Tameka and I had my oldest son and even though it wasn't going too good for us during the pregnancy, we got pregnant and had another son exactly 1 year after our 1st son was born! I was beginning to understand what Zohra was going through. She wasn't a monster or a bad person…she was a person who didn't make wise choices in life like all of us have done.

Her choices early on in life led her to having multiple kids given up for adoption, but there's a flipside. In this letter, she let me know her thoughts on abortion. At one point, she viewed me as being a cancer in her body that she wanted to get rid of. Abortion would get rid of this "cancer" in a society-approved way.

Was she a horrible person for thinking about killing me and not letting me breath a breath of fresh air? No. Her letting me in on that information only brought us closer.

During my lifetime, I made the decision with 2 females to kill our children. To simplify it, I was directly involved with the murder of 2 of my children. Not "abortions". That is a light term that hides what it is.

Using the term "abortion" instead of 1st degree murder is like calling someone "gay" instead of saying the person is involved in homosexual activity. Abortion is a misleading term and a process that both my mother and I had contemplated in our lives.

My mother, thank God, did not carry out her murderous thoughts of killing me in her body. She allowed me to participate in this thing we call life and for that, I have to admit she was in fact a better parent than I was! How could I be mad at her?

Her and I were faced with similar situations and she took a morally higher path and put me up for adoption; while I took the easier, immoral path of murdering my own children! This letter allowed me to not only take a look at her from a different viewpoint, it also made me take a deep look at my own life choices, both from a parent and adopted child view.

With her letter, I had finally arrived. I had arrived at the place where yes, I have a white mom and a black mom and yes, I love them both. Do I love them equally? I have to honestly say that I don't.

I love my white mom in a way that is based on appreciation. My love for her is based on her making a conscious decision to commit her life to raising me to adulthood as though I came from her womb...and she stuck with that commitment...and I love her for that...and I always will love her for that...and even though she is my white mom, I will take it as a sign of disrespect if you say anything bad out my mom!

I love my black mom that is based on genetics. My love for her is based on her making a conscious decision to put me in a situation where I would have a better chance of enjoying a higher quality of living than she could offer me at that point and time in our lives.

Her decision to both act in a sexually irresponsible manner and put me up for adoption allowed me to be in the perfect and ideal position in life where God can use me to establish Heaven on Earth, as is His purpose for us that Jesus expressed when He said, "...may your Kingdom come and may your Will be done **on Earth like it is in Heaven...**"

To both of my moms, I have to let the world know I love you both in our own way.

To both of my moms, I have to let the world know that I am thankful for appreciate both of your parenting styles.

To you the reader, I have to let you know this chapter is over, so keep reading. CHAPTER FOUR will be just as informative and often times as off-track as the previous 3 chapters were...

CHAPTER FOUR

<u>Being a Dad</u>

I was adopted at birth into a white family. I was beginning to understand the different family structures in America that white families had versus black families. There were definite differences...not excuses or claims to support racial superiority. Just differences.

With my awareness of these differences, I should have been more aggressive in making sure that 1) my kids had a dad and break the historical, detrimental effects of slavery on the black family structure and 2) if I did have children, I needed to intentionally focus on getting myself in the best position possible to take care of them. I failed at both of those objectives...

My journey to becoming a dad, and mostly that was in the capacity of a baby daddy, wasn't intentional, but it became a situation I was not ashamed of. Remember, I was trying to live out my version of what I thought a black man and father was based on movies, local news broadcast and from what I observed in my circles of society.

After I messed up the relationship with my oldest kid's mom, I was officially a Baby Daddy. In my eyes, I wasn't trippin'. The black men I saw on the news had kids by different women and called the women "baby mama" and they in turn called the father of their children "baby daddy".

In my view, I was following black-man protocol. In all fairness to black men in general, my journey to find black, male role models wasn't in corporate America. I had heard my biological dad was a big, muscular guy who grew up always fighting and I wanted to go that route.

Once I got that information, I took that and morphed it with my complete hatred for white males and their system of American government and became Nino. That was my nickname. It came from a movie called "New Jack City". In that movie, the main character was a big drug-dealer named Nino Brown.

In that movie, he took over a huge apartment complex and ran the majority of his multi-million-dollar drug operation from there. Since I was that guy you could call on to help evict people from your property, I got the nickname Nino. Anyways...

That mentality took me to the streets. I wanted to run the streets and be "black", so that's what I did. I began to run cocaine from Texas to Michigan. I was involved with gunplay. I went to jail a couple of times for stolen cars and once for threatening somebody with a gun. That case was dropped because they couldn't find the gun and the person didn't show up. I only went to prison once for a year due to a gun-possession case.

The other 20 times I went to county jails stemmed from child support. I was what they called a dead-beat dad. I had baby mamas in several states and wasn't supporting any of them financially. I didn't care. The guys I hung around with didn't care. The common mentality in my crowd was that I had to do what I had to do to get money 1st and after that, do my best to take care of my children.

I may have distorted it and gave it my own twist and decided to do very little financial support and only give my time...as best I could. By that, I meant I would see my kids when it was convenient for me. When I wasn't selling drugs or doing drugs, I would have days where I would seek out opportunities to spend time with them.

I wasn't interested in doing anything productive in terms of family life. There were guys I would hustle with or party with and they made sure to spend time and money with their kids. They didn't want their kids to have to live the street life like they had to.

For me it was different because I chose street life...it didn't choose me and because of that, I wasn't concerned with my kids entering that lifestyle or being forced to sell drugs. All of my kids had stable moms who were able to, not by choice, be that strong, black woman and mama.

This was a very selfish period of my life. I didn't care about anybody else's feelings or what they were going through in life. It was all about me and my search to become a black man in America.

Once I got back into the Bible, I grew up in the church, my view changed. This was the period where I began to give a damn. I was able to stop searching and start living.

I had tried to be white. I had tried to be black. I had tried to experience life with a black mom. I had tried to be like my biological dad or at least what I thought he must have been like. I was exhausted. Exhausted but finally able to experience long periods of drug-free time where I could get to know my children.

It was time for me to try something new and that new thing was fatherhood. I had a taste of it for a while with 2 of my younger kids. They each lived with their moms but me and both of their moms had something like a visitation schedule that allowed for me to spend weekends with the kids at their mom's house and spend time with them whenever I was clean and sober.

As I tried my hand at being a dad, my thoughts kept going to Zohra. Would my kids be better off if I had adopted them? What if I had never had them? What would I be doing? What if I never killed 2 of my children via abortion?

I wasn't doing too good at the whole dad thing until I got the letter from Zohra. Once I was able to view her as a person who made "good" and "bad" choices like we all do in life, I was able to understand her and accept her with all of her "goods" and "bads". That's what I wanted from my kids. If I was going to be their dad, I would have to reset the clock and that meant writing them "It wasn't you" letters like the one Zohra had written.

I didn't literally write letters to my kids, but I did begin to have some talks. These talks have gotten us a lot closer and a lot farther at the same time. Regardless of the direction it took my relationships with my kids, I have to say, opening up and letting your kids look at your life and see that you are human makes a big difference.

Both of my wife's parents were addicted to drugs and alcohol and both of them caught AIDS. As she watched me go through my addiction drama, she began to ask herself how her relationship would have been different if she was able to take the time to ask her parents why they made the decisions they had made.

Some things she says she would have asked mom were, "Why did you start doing drugs?" and "Did being adopted affect your attitude in life" and "Why did you have kids knowing you were in the midst of some heavy addictions?"

There was the same basic line of questioning she would have asked her dad as well. The bottom line for her was that she saw from my life and addictions some of the things she wished she had known about her parents. Maybe she could have loved them on a deeper level. Maybe she could have been more sympathetic to their lifestyles. Maybe, maybe, maybe...

As I began to explain to my kids that I wasn't a good dad to them because I was addicted to sniffing coke and smoking crack, they were able to decide for themselves how to address it. They were able to decide whether they wanted to still love me or write me off as a dead-beat dad, a loser by society's standards or as a crackhead.

Our "It wasn't you" conversations paved the way for father-child relationships that had substance. Letting my children know that me not being there for them had zero to do with them gave us all a freedom to love another human unconditionally.

I hadn't realized it until I opened myself up to my children that this was what I had been searching for all along! I had been so busy trying to be black and white and thugged out and doped up that I was missing the obvious: I wanted unconditional love!

As I continued on my drug-free path in life, my walk with God became a necessity. Let me clarify something really quick. When I say "my walk with God became a necessity" what I should have said was "my DAILY walk with God became a necessity."

For me, understanding and believing that God was behind all of the design, law and order we see in life made the difference for me from wanting to be a man to wanting to be a man who was capable of giving and receiving love unconditionally.

Everything was complete for me. I had my white mom and dad and I had knowledge of my black dad and had a solid relationship now with my black mom. I also had a stable, productive, loving relationship with my spiritual Father. It was this relationship that taught me how to apply unconditional love to my other relationships.

I was able to learn from my spiritual Father things that society, drugs, sex and money could never teach me and I was complete. I had become a dad, made in the image of my Heavenly Father.

SUMMARY

Summary. Summary. Summary. Sometimes I feel the need for them and other times I don't. In this case I feel the need for a brief summary.

Since the sub-title of this book is "an Adoption Story", I hope you the reader has been able to get an inside picture of what adoption is, or at least can be, like from an array of angles. It will not always be a pretty picture and sometimes the child and the biological parent may never meet.

In either case, my closing thought for anyone who is affected by adoption in any way would be this:

You are who you are regardless of your relationship with your parents. Whether you believe it or not, you always had and will always have a Heavenly Father who has a plan for you. Please take the time to study the Bible and the Lost Books of the Bible for yourself to find your very own, unique, customized plan and purpose for your life. Don't do it for your culture. Don't do it for your political party and don't do it for your kids...they all change and come and go. Do it for God and for yourself.

The last section has a couple of Private Matter Bonus Essays. These topics deal with the book in some way or other and are topics that people tend to shy away from talking about in public. Not me. I'd rather get the discussion it out in the open so it can't hide in the dark and keep people locked in shame and guilt. Check 'em out:

ABORTION

Why is there such a big debate about abortion and when human life starts? This has got to be one of the stupidest debates in the world and that's why I don't get into that discussion. I may shoot off this Private Matter essay and that's about it.

Let me simplify a couple of key points for you:

1. **When does human life start?** Human life starts when a man and a woman have sex and she gets pregnant. Wasn't that simple? When a man and woman have sex and she gets pregnant, a human has started its' life. Oh wait, some of you may have been thinking that a man and a woman can have sex and create a whale? Or a horse? Maybe a rhinoceros? I mean, come on, people. Debating when a human life starts is a simple question and answer thing. We don't need the world's top "thinkers" to help us in the discussion of when human life starts. There has to be more to it than just that...

2. **Is abortion 1ˢᵗ Degree murder?** Yes. Once again, pretty straight-forward here, people. If murder is when you make a plan to kill somebody and you carry it out…that's 1ˢᵗ Degree murder. Quick question for you: When you decided to kill the baby, was it planned out in anyway? Did you maybe call Planned Parenthood, give them your information, set up an appointment, got a reminder text the morning of, came in for the appointment and had the baby killed? If so, I'm gonna have to say that's 1ˢᵗ Degree murder. Here's another simple example for you: I get mad at a guy who stole my girlfriend. I know the bar where he likes to have a few drinks. He likes to get there at around 6pm and leaves around midnight. He doesn't live far from there, so he walks. I know his exact route. Just to make sure, I watch him for 3 nights. On the 4ᵗʰ night, I casually walk up behind him and quickly let off 2 shots, point-blank in the base of his head with a snub-nose, .38 Special and slowly slip into the car parked near the spot and my friends drives off. He's dead before he hits the ground. Everything works as planned. Is that 1ˢᵗ Degree murder? If it is, then abortion is murder.

3. **Is it the woman's right to kill the child?** Yes. Since the baby is inside the woman and she's the one who is going to start eating some pretty nasty food combinations, have her nose, feet, knees and ankles get swollen and sore…and let's not forget there will be something living inside her that will be growing, eating and shitting in her…I would *definitely* say she has the choice whether to let the baby human live or kill it.

Since the answers to these questions are extremely simple and straightforward, there has to be something behind the curtain when it deals with abortion. The key is to figure out what the fuck it is so we can stop wasting time with distractions and start using our efforts to enjoy life and stop killing it.

I'm going to suggest that it's a combination of guilt and Satan. I'll do the guilt part 1st because once you mention Satan, people don't know what to do or say. Is he real? Is he as bad as the Bible says? Does he really have the power to influence society? Getting back to the topic of guilt…

There is a growing trend in society to baby people. I'm not talking about little kids; I'm talking about treating grown-ass people like little kids.

The word "retard" means slow or slower. If there is a person whose brain is not developing at the rate it should to allow him or her to function as an adult, he or she is classified as being mentally retarded…not a "retard" or "retarded." See the difference?

One statement is a cold, by-the-book fact talking about a person's trait or characteristic; while the other is a label that takes away from a person's human value and is unacceptable for people to use…*especially* Believers.

How does this relate to abortion? When you pre-plan and carry out the death of an unborn baby, you are guilty of 1st Degree murder. That does NOT mean you are a murderer. It means you are a person who committed the crime of murder. Yes, you are guilty of that crime; but you are still a person who can 1) take responsibility for the crime of murder, 2) have the guilt aspect of it taken away and 3) you are not a bad, evil person.

People are trying to allow a mother-to-be to kill her child without the guilt. It doesn't work that way. Anyone guilty of a crime is guilty. A crime is a crime and guilt is guilt.

Let's talk about Satan and abortion. I will be brief because if you're interested in this topic more, you can read the book, "Safe Sex Saves Satan."

I do want to say Satan is a real being and it is proven that he hates humans. Why? Because he is a being who used to be one of the top-dogs in Heaven and got kicked out and can NEVER return to that blessed, powerful state of living.

His only goal now, and he put this on the public record for everyone to see, is to make sure humans don't get to enjoy Heaven on Earth or the spiritual realm known as Heaven. We are his eternal enemies.

What if...what if he *is* able to influence people? I mean, what if he was able to influence people to kill their babies? Wouldn't that help him accomplish his main goal?

Abortion serves Satan *extremely* well:

1. **Abortion kills humans. Every baby that gets murdered is one less human that can enjoy Heaven…just the way he wants it.**
2. **Abortion creates guilt. Every woman I know who has killed her growing baby has, on some level, had guilt. It's a natural reaction to have guilt after killing a baby. A female can say, "Yeah, girl. I just did what I had to do." Sounds good, but there's guilt. Anytime you live with guilt, it makes it hard for you to guide someone else in life. How can you tell your daughter to have responsible sex…when you had irresponsible sex that led to you killing a baby?**
3. **Abortion is a distraction. Do you know how much time and resources we waste on this abortion shit? How about we start focusing on responsible sex??? We do that and there's no more abortion!!**

Yes, I have been involved in abortions. 2 to be exact.

Yes, I have lived with the guilt of it and it makes me

hesitant to tell my kids, or anybody for that matter, to have

responsible sex…when I've had irresponsible sex that has led to

the death of two babies.

Yes, I didn't feel right talking about responsible sex until I

got into the Bible and allowed God to help me deal with the guilt

of it all.

Oh! I just thought about something! Since abortion is 1st degree murder, shouldn't the person be charged with murder? Why isn't the mother and father charged with murder? If they are charged with murder, what should the punishment be? People get prison time for neglecting a dog or cat...so why shouldn't the parents get prison time? And if so, how far back can you go to charge somebody with the crime of abortion?

That's just something I had on my mind that I wanted to share publicly that a lot of us have talked about in private that needs to be discussed publicly.

A Woman's Worth

The Bible has several examples of how a woman can use her natural power and the results she can command:

Intentional use of Power: Jacob's mother used her female power of persuasion to help him deceive his father; Esther used her beauty and charm to become a queen and save her Jewish culture from genocide; the daughter of Herodias performed a sexual dance for the King who was so aroused by it that he told her she could have up to half of his kingdom; King David was about to kill a man and all the man's sons for disrespecting him but the man's wife stepped in and appeased David and saved her husband's life; God was going to kill Moses until his wife stepped in and did what God had wanted and that act saved Moses' life; and then there was King Solomon who asked God for wisdom over everything and in the end he allowed his wives to lead him astray to the point where he built temples for them to worship foreign gods and idols.

Unintentional use of Power: King David *looked* at a woman and wanted her so bad that he had her husband murdered; Jacob saw a beautiful female and told her dad that he would work for him for free for 7 years if he could marry her...he was tricked and forced to marry her older sister, but he went and told the dad he would *still* work for 7 more years if he could marry the younger sister who he wanted in the beginning; in Genesis it was told that the angels in Heaven *looked* down at the women on Earth and wanted them so badly that they would rather live on Earth and have them than live in Heaven; and finally, David had a son who lusted after his own step-sister so badly that he became physically sick and eventually raped her.

Understanding the worth of a woman and her role in a man's life is crucial, both from the man's point of view and the woman's. On several occasions God warned different men about their selection of a wife because if a wife doesn't love God, she has the power to lead her husband away from God. The first example of this was in the Garden of Eden. The apostle Paul says

that sometimes it's best if a man stays single because a married

man has a hard time pleasing God because of his strong, natural

desire to please his wife. And at the same time, there

At the same time, the Bible mentions how a man should

find a good wife because she will complement him and they will

both be happy and powerful. In the Garden of Eden, Eve was

created because God determined that Adam needed a female

companion to complete him.

Here are some Bible verses that talk some more about a

woman's worth:

1. Proverbs 11:16 – a kindhearted woman gains honor

2. Genesis 2:24 – a man will leave his parents to be with a

   woman

3. Proverbs 31:10-31 – a wife of noble character is:

   worth more than rubies, she has strength and dignity,

gives good advice, helps the poor and deserves honor

for everything that she does…

4. Proverbs 18:22 - Whoever finds a wife finds something

    that is good and receives favor from God.

5. Psalm 68:5 – God is a protector of widows

6. Exodus 22:22 – God says He will kill anyone who takes

    advantage of widows

7. Proverbs 12:24 – a disgraceful wife is like decay in her

    husband's bones

8. Proverbs 19:13 – a quarrelsome wife is like a constant

    drip from a leaky roof

9. Proverbs 29:3 – whoever messes with prostitutes will

    be poor

10. Proverbs 6:26 – an adulterous wife will cost you your

    life

11. Ecclesiastes 7:26 – thoughts of getting trapped by a

    woman are worse than contemplating death

In the end, a woman has the support life or death. She needs no weapons of war. Her mind, beauty and natural feminine qualities are her weapons of choice. How a woman follows instructions and where she gets her instructions from determines her worth and value.

The Bible: Basis Instructions Before Leaving Earth

Cross-Cultural Advantage

Culture is a major part of being human. It is, at bare minimum, the common link between any two people. It gives a person pride in their country. It gives any given group in society a feeling of purpose and accomplishment. Culture is what gives you a basis for your existence. Cultural festivals are proud moments for anyone of the group being celebrated; especially when the celebration is world-wide. For people without cultural identity, any cultural benefits are un-applicable to you. Characteristics of people in "culture-less" groups tend to be lack of motivation, anger, jealousy, stress, depression, isolation, self-hatred and their actions typically appear to have been programmed and controlled by negative outside forces.

The highest levels of joy and beauty in life can only be found in opposites. You appreciate summer's heat after experiencing winter's cool. You appreciate and strive for the feeling of being loved and acknowledged more so after being hated and ignored. Seeing the sun sets your mind on a different mentality after being able to shut down and relax hours earlier under the cloak of darkness. Humanity began and exists because of opposites: the sexual actions and differences of a man and a woman. When you have no other connections to humans and feel isolated it's gratifying to be able to know and build on cultural connections to give you that feeling of being a part of something.

Culture is a major part of being human. It is, at bare minimum, the common link between any two people. When that bare minimum desire of humanity does not exist, purpose in life gets distorted.

The Bible introduces us to a new culture. A culture that is 100% positive. Something that is 100% means there is no room for anything else. It is full. It is complete; and in the case of the cross culture there is no room for negativity such as lack of motivation, anger, jealousy, stress, depression, isolation and self-hatred. This culture is symbolized by the cross: the act of Jesus dying on the cross. That act introduced us to the only culture that matters.

Being a part of the Cross Culture has benefits with no liabilities. When you are a part of that culture, you interact with people differently. You don't judge someone based on their appearance, because you understand appearances don't determine achievable elevation in life. You understand that *everyone* has the same seed-potential as you. You are governed by laws that transcend every manmade law that is not based on or enforced with love.

The only outside influences in this culture are God. Your understanding of and getting into relationship with God is what gives members of this culture an advantage over any other cultural group. Every cultural group except for Cross Culture is limited by ethnicity or acceptance by a member of a certain ethnicity. Cross Culture is only limited by humanity without distinction. Meaning, each member is a distinct, valuable member of this culture with the only qualification being that you are a human.

Worldly kings and queens are crowned based on money and bloodlines. Cross Culture kings and queens are crowned at birth regardless of their economic status or bloodline at birth. Cross Culture members have the inalienable right by birth to be the first in a line of royalty in their bloodline at any point and time in their life. Cross Culture kings and queens are proclaimed royalty by the creator of the universe...not by the amount of wealth his family has or by the inherited status of his or her parents. Money can be manipulated and so can royalty that is based on it; bloodlines have no bearing in determining admission to royalty of a Cross Culture member.

A Cross Culture member is only limited in life by his or her view on what Jesus did by dying on the cross: Your view matters.

BIBLE: Basic Instructions Before Leaving Earth

Personal Development Notes

69

Personal Development Notes

Personal Development Notes

Personal Development Notes

Personal Development Notes